HAL•LEONARD
INSTRUMENTAL
PLAY-ALONG

CLARINET

T0070466

Christmas SONGS

CONTENTS

To access audio visit:
www.halleonard.com/mylibrary

Enter Code
5916-4967-8302-9268

Audio Arrangements by Peter Deneff

ISBN 978-1-4950-2553-2

HAL•LEONARD®
CORPORATION
7777 W. BLUEMOUND RD. P.O. BOX 13819 MILWAUKEE, WI 53213

Visit Hal Leonard Online at
www.halleonard.com

ALL I WANT FOR CHRISTMAS IS YOU

Clarinet

Words and Music by MARIAH CAREY
and WALTER AFANASIEFF

THE CHRISTMAS WALTZ

CLARINET

Words by SAMMY CAHN
Music by JULE STYNE

HAPPY HOLIDAY

from the Motion Picture Irving Berlin's HOLIDAY INN

Clarinet

Words and Music by
IRVING BERLIN

I WONDER AS I WANDER

CLARINET

By JOHN JACOB NILES

I'LL BE HOME FOR CHRISTMAS

Clarinet

Words and Music by KIM GANNON
and WALTER KENT

LET IT SNOW! LET IT SNOW! LET IT SNOW!

CLARINET

Words by SAMMY CAHN
Music by JULE STYNE

MARY, DID YOU KNOW?

Clarinet

Words and Music by MARK LOWRY
and BUDDY GREENE

THE MOST WONDERFUL TIME OF THE YEAR

CLARINET

Words and Music by EDDIE POLA
and GEORGE WYLE

MY FAVORITE THINGS
from THE SOUND OF MUSIC

Clarinet

Lyrics by OSCAR HAMMERSTEIN II
Music by RICHARD RODGERS

SILVER BELLS

from the Paramount Picture THE LEMON DROP KID

Clarinet

Words and Music by JAY LIVINGSTON
and RAY EVANS

THIS CHRISTMAS

Clarinet

Words and Music by DONNY HATHAWAY
and NADINE McKINNOR

WHITE CHRISTMAS

from the Motion Picture Irving Berlin's HOLIDAY INN

CLARINET

Words and Music by
IRVING BERLIN

HAL•LEONARD INSTRUMENTAL PLAY-ALONG

Your favorite songs are arranged just for solo instrumentalists with this outstanding series. Each book includes a great full-accompaniment play-along CD so you can sound just like a pro! Check out www.halleonard.com to see all the titles available.

Disney Greats
Arabian Nights • Hawaiian Roller Coaster Ride • It's a Small World • Look Through My Eyes • Yo Ho (A Pirate's Life for Me) • and more.

	00841934	Flute	$12.95
	00841935	Clarinet	$12.95
	00841936	Alto Sax	$12.95
	00841937	Tenor Sax	$12.95
	00841938	Trumpet	$12.95
	00841939	Horn	$12.95
	00841940	Trombone	$12.95
	00841941	Violin	$12.95
	00841942	Viola	$12.95
	00841943	Cello	$12.95
	00842078	Oboe	$12.95

Great Themes
Bella's Lullaby • Chariots of Fire • Get Smart • Hawaii Five-O Theme • I Love Lucy • The Odd Couple • Spanish Flea • and more.

	00842468	Flute	$12.99
	00842469	Clarinet	$12.99
	00842470	Alto Sax	$12.99
	00842471	Tenor Sax	$12.99
	00842472	Trumpet	$12.99
	00842473	Horn	$12.99
	00842474	Trombone	$12.99
	00842475	Violin	$12.99
	00842476	Viola	$12.99
	00842477	Cello	$12.99

Coldplay
Clocks • Every Teardrop Is a Waterfall • Fix You • In My Place • Lost! • Paradise • The Scientist • Speed of Sound • Trouble • Violet Hill • Viva La Vida • Yellow.

	00103337	Flute	$12.99
	00103338	Clarinet	$12.99
	00103339	Alto Sax	$12.99
	00103340	Tenor Sax	$12.99
	00103341	Trumpet	$12.99
	00103342	Horn	$12.99
	00103343	Trombone	$12.99
	00103344	Violin	$12.99
	00103345	Viola	$12.99
	00103346	Cello	$12.99

Popular Hits
Breakeven • Fireflies • Halo • Hey, Soul Sister • I Gotta Feeling • I'm Yours • Need You Now • Poker Face • Viva La Vida • You Belong with Me • and more.

	00842511	Flute	$12.99
	00842512	Clarinet	$12.99
	00842513	Alto Sax	$12.99
	00842514	Tenor Sax	$12.99
	00842515	Trumpet	$12.99
	00842516	Horn	$12.99
	00842517	Trombone	$12.99
	00842518	Violin	$12.99
	00842519	Viola	$12.99
	00842520	Cello	$12.99

Lennon & McCartney Favorites
All You Need Is Love • A Hard Day's Night • Here, There and Everywhere • Hey Jude • Let It Be • Nowhere Man • Penny Lane • She Loves You • When I'm Sixty-Four • and more.

	00842600	Flute	$12.99
	00842601	Clarinet	$12.99
	00842602	Alto Sax	$12.99
	00842603	Tenor Sax	$12.99
	00842604	Trumpet	$12.99
	00842605	Horn	$12.99
	00842606	Trombone	$12.99
	00842607	Violin	$12.99
	00842608	Viola	$12.99
	00842609	Cello	$12.99

Women of Pop
Bad Romance • Jar of Hearts • Mean • My Life Would Suck Without You • Our Song • Rolling in the Deep • Single Ladies (Put a Ring on It) • Teenage Dream • and more.

	00842650	Flute	$12.99
	00842651	Clarinet	$12.99
	00842652	Alto Sax	$12.99
	00842653	Tenor Sax	$12.99
	00842654	Trumpet	$12.99
	00842655	Horn	$12.99
	00842656	Trombone	$12.99
	00842657	Violin	$12.99
	00842658	Viola	$12.99
	00842659	Cello	$12.99

Movie Music
And All That Jazz • Come What May • I Am a Man of Constant Sorrow • I Believe I Can Fly • I Walk the Line • Seasons of Love • Theme from *Spider Man* • and more.

	00842090	Clarinet	$10.95
	00842091	Alto Sax	$10.95
	00842092	Tenor Sax	$10.95
	00842094	Horn	$10.95
	00842095	Trombone	$10.95
	00842096	Violin	$10.95
	00842097	Viola	$10.95

TV Favorites
The Addams Family Theme • The Brady Bunch • Green Acres Theme • Happy Days • Johnny's Theme • Linus and Lucy • Theme from the Simpsons • and more.

	00842079	Flute	$10.95
	00842080	Clarinet	$10.95
	00842081	Alto Sax	$10.95
	00842082	Tenor Sax	$10.95
	00842083	Trumpet	$10.95
	00842084	Horn	$10.95
	00842085	Trombone	$10.95
	00842087	Viola	$10.95

Wicked
As Long As You're Mine • Dancing Through Life • Defying Gravity • For Good • I'm Not That Girl • Popular • The Wizard and I • and more.

	00842236	Flute	$11.95
	00842237	Clarinet	$11.95
	00842238	Alto Saxophone	$11.95
	00842239	Tenor Saxophone	$11.95
	00842240	Trumpet	$11.95
	00842241	Horn	$11.95
	00842242	Trombone	$11.95
	00842243	Violin	$11.95
	00842244	Viola	$11.95
	00842245	Cello	$11.95

FOR MORE INFORMATION, SEE YOUR LOCAL MUSIC DEALER, OR WRITE TO:

HAL•LEONARD® CORPORATION
7777 W. BLUEMOUND RD. P.O. BOX 13819 MILWAUKEE, WI 53213